S0-BNT-968

LAUNDRY
HINTS & TIPS

LAUNDRY
HINTS & TIPS

CINDY HARRIS

RYLAND PETERS & SMALL
LONDON • NEW YORK

Senior Designer Toni Kay
Commissioning Editor Stephanie Milner
Head of Production Patricia Harrington
Picture Manager Christina Borsi
Art Director Leslie Harrington
Editorial Director Julia Charles

First published in 2005.
This edition published in 2014
by Ryland Peters & Small
20–21 Jockey's Fields
London WC1R 4BW
and
519 Broadway, 5th Floor
New York, NY 10012
www.rylandpeters.com

10 9 8 7 6 5 4 3 2

Text © Cindy Harris 2005, 2014
Design and photographs © Ryland Peters &
Small 2014

ISBN 978-1-84975-579-5

A CIP record for this book is
available from the British Library.

Library of Congress CIP data has been
applied for.

Printed and bound in China

CONTENTS

INTRODUCTION

How inviting it is to climb into a freshly-laundered bed or to wrap yourself up in a clean, fluffy towel after luxuriating in the bath? Isn't it far more appealing to have a freshly-pressed pile of clothes to choose from in the morning instead of pulling on a crumpled shirt off the floor as you rush out the door? These are the easy-to-achieve results that should help transform your laundry routine from a chore into a pleasure.

With little effort you can turn your home into a tactile heaven – sweet-smelling clothes and linens, piles of folded, fluffy towels and crisply-pressed shirts – giving results that will make you both proud and satisfied. From washing and drying to ironing, pressing and folding, this book will help you rediscover these simple pleasures in life.

GETTING STARTED

Bed linen, table linen, towels and clothes: laundry can seem a never-ending chore. However, if you approach it in a methodical way and have some good accessories to help you, you will start off on the right foot and make the task simple and easier to deal with.

GETTING TO GRIPS WITH YOUR LAUNDRY

The best way to deal with your household's laundry, and to maintain your sanity in the process, is to do the majority of the washing on a designated day. That way you won't be burdened with wet shirts, towels or sheets every single day of the week and you can tackle the ironing when you have a free half hour.

The Basics

• Schedule a major laundry day once a week. If you have a busy work schedule or want to keep your weekends free, you may need to do a few loads during the week.

• Put a laundry basket/hamper, or three-way sorter in each bedroom or bathroom.

• If you have the space it's a good idea to have separate laundry baskets/hampers for whites and lights, coloureds and darks and delicates or hand-washables.

• Separate out items that need to be dry-cleaned and put them in a closet bag.

• It's always best to treat a stain as soon as possible. However, if you are unable to get to the stain immediately, indicate its location with a safety pin before putting the item in the laundry basket, so you can find it again easily.

• If your clothes need hemming, darning or repairing in any way, do so before washing as laundering may enlarge the tears.

• Do a full load of towels only. This will use less water, less energy and restrict lint.

• If you are using a tumble dryer, dry loads one after the other to utilize the remaining heat from the previous load.

• Always fold clothes before transporting them.

• Leave lone socks in a bag in the laundry/utility room to match with its mate later.

• Keep a few wooden, padded and rubber-clip hangers handy in the laundry/utility room or near the tumble dryer, so you can hang easily-creased items immediately after drying. This will help to prevent wrinkles from forming.

• Return wire hangers to the dry-cleaners or throw them out. Don't use them to hang up your clothes because they can ruin the shape of garments.

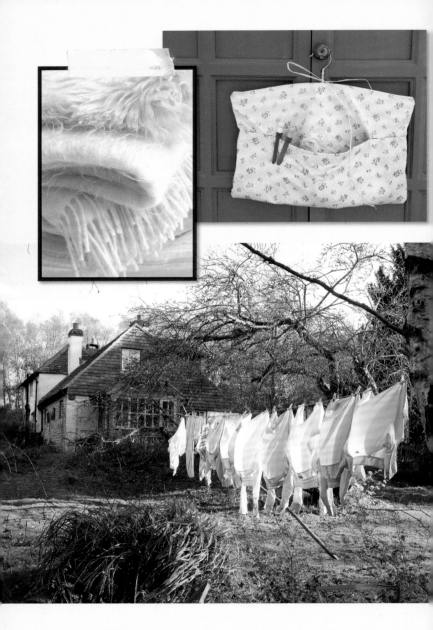

HOW OFTEN SHOULD YOU LAUNDER?

Try to do a little bit of laundry – whether it's washing, drying or ironing – twice a week, before it becomes an overwhelming chore. A brimming ironing or laundry basket/hamper is easier to ignore. However, to save fuel and water, wait until you have a full load before firing the washing machine into action.

Daily
• Socks and underwear should be put in the laundry after each use.
• Most other items of clothing can be worn at least twice, as long as there are no stains or odours.
• Dish towels may need to be changed on a daily basis if you cook frequently. Otherwise, change them a couple of times a week.

Twice a Week
• Change bath towels.

Once a Week
• Change bed linen once a week, unless the person is ill when you should change it more frequently.
• Put pillows to tumble dry for about 15 minutes to freshen them and to eliminate dust mites.

A Few Times a Year
• Launder all additional bed linen including mattress covers, blankets, cushion/pillow covers, quilts and duvets/comforters at least once every three months.
• Turn most frequently used mattresses every four to six months – flip from top to bottom as well as from side to side. Vacuum the mattresses when you flip them.
• Launder pillows according to the instructions on the labels.

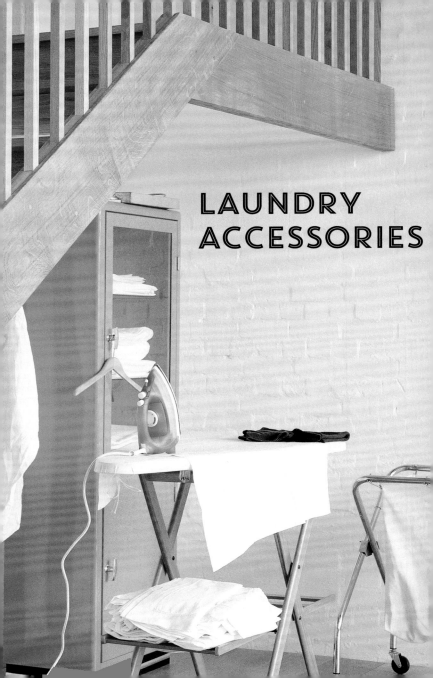

LAUNDRY
ACCESSORIES

* Wooden or plastic-coated *concertina drying rack* for use in periods of wet weather or to dry clothes that can't be tumble dried.

* Folding *laundry basket/hamper*.

* *Clothes roller* to remove fluff and lint from clothes.

* *Net washing bags* to keep small items together or protect delicates.

* *Hanger of pegs* for socks and handkerchiefs.

* *Iron* and *ironing board*.

* *Water spray bottle* for ironing.

* *Iron soleplate cleaner*.

* *Fold-flat ironing valets* to hang up clothes once they are ironed.

* *Multi-tidy baskets* or a *rolling caddy* for storing a sewing kit, shoe polish, spot removers, cloths, paper towels, household hint books and so on.

* *Container* to empty pocket contents into before washing.

* *Waistband stretchers* to dry trousers/pants and make creases.

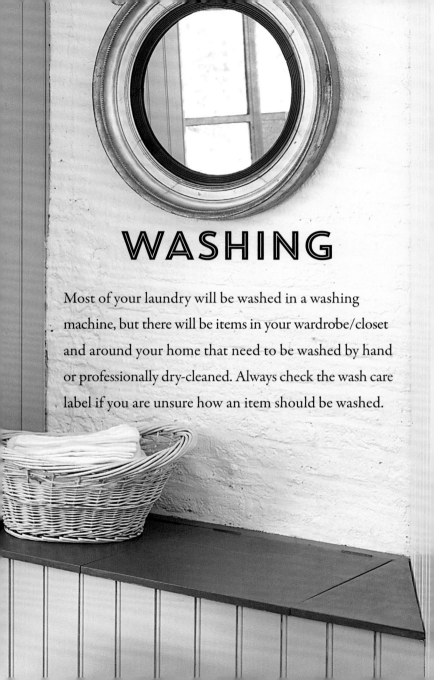

WASHING

Most of your laundry will be washed in a washing machine, but there will be items in your wardrobe/closet and around your home that need to be washed by hand or professionally dry-cleaned. Always check the wash care label if you are unsure how an item should be washed.

WASHING MACHINES

There are two types of washing machine: front-loading and top-loading. Front-loading machines consume less energy and less water than their top-loading counterparts. The most popular type of machines are front-loading automatics, which can wash around 5 kg/11 lbs., but there is a growing trend for larger capacity machines that can wash up to 8 kg/17½ lbs. In Europe, all laundry appliances are required by law to carry an EU energy label which gives details of energy and water consumption, efficiency and noise level. For optimum performance, read the manufacturer's instructions to make sure you use the right programme for each load and follow the instructions here.

The Basics

- Select the appropriate programme on your machine to correspond to the type of fabric you are washing. Make sure you have selected the right programme, temperature and spin speed if the controls are separate. Don't forget to check the options available such as extra rinse, delicate or rapid wash.

- Load the drum (taking care not to overload), add the detergent and fabric conditioner to the dispenser or put the detergent directly into the drum using a dosing ball. Switch on the machine and it will stop once the cycle is complete.

- Don't machine wash items that should be hand-washed or dry-cleaned. Always check the wash care labels on garments first.

- For heavy or oily stains, use a liquid pre-wash treatment first.

- Use as high a temperature programme as possible to remove heavy stains, but don't exceed the temperature recommended for individual items.

- Use a lower temperature and reduced agitation programme (indicated by a solid or broken bar under the washing machine symbol on care labels) to reduce shrinking and fading and to pre-soak hard-to-remove stains, such as blood and food.

- Match the detergent to the fabric and level of staining.

- Use in-wash stain removers or optical brighteners to whiten, brighten and clean.

- Proprietary whitening products will help remove yellowing on whites. Alternatively pre-soak them in a bleach solution.

- Use liquid fabric softener in the final rinse, or add a dryer sheet to your tumble dryer, to reduce static cling and make your clothes softer.

- Add liquid starch to the final rinse for crispness.

- Clean the washing machine every few months to get clothes cleaner. Select the 95°C (200°F) cycle, add 250 ml/1 cup of white vinegar to the detergent dispenser and run an empty cycle.

- Check hoses yearly for cracks and bubbles. Replace as needed to avoid leaks.

- Clean washer filters periodically and dryer filters after each load.

GUIDE TO WASH CARE SYMBOLS CHART

SQUARE	CIRCLE	IRON	TRIANGLE	WASHTUB
Drying	*Dry-cleaning*	*Ironing*	*Bleaching*	*Washing*
item may be tumble dried (no heat): solid lines beneath this symbol indicate press functions	**dry-clean using any type of solvent**	**hot iron:** a maximum temperature of 210°C (390°F) may be used	**chlorine bleach may be used**	**cotton wash:** normal (maximum) washing conditions can be used at the appropriate temperature, in this case 60°C
tumble dry (low heat): several dots indicate higher heat settings	**dry-clean in any solvent, except trichloroethylene**	**warm iron:** a maximum temperature of 160°C (300°F) may be used	**do not use chlorine bleach**	**synthetics/ permanent wash:** reduced (medium) washing conditions apply
do not tumble dry	**dry-clean with petroleum solvent only**	**cool iron:** a maximum temperature of 120°C (230°F) may be used	**use any bleach**	**wool/delicate wash:** much reduced (minimum) washing conditions to be used. Applies specifically to machine-washable wool products
line dry				
drip dry				
dry flat	**do not dry-clean**	**do not iron**	**use only non-chlorine bleach**	**hand-wash:** do not machine wash
do not wring		**do not steam**		**do not wash**

WASHING MACHINE CYCLES

Washing machines have a huge range of programmes and washing options to choose from. The following three programmes are the most common.

Cotton/Regular A heavy duty programme (maximum/fast agitation) for cotton, denim and linen fabrics. The most common temperatures are 40°C (105°F) for light soiling and delicate cottons; 60°C (140°F) for heavier soils; and 95°C (200°F) for very heavy stains and for destroying germs. Some machines will automatically set the temperature while others have a separate temperature control. Use strong, all-purpose detergent in this cycle. Hot water is effective at removing stains most thoroughly, but it can shrink and fade your laundry. Select this program with caution.

Synthetic/Permanent (easy-care) Suitable for man-made fabrics such as polyester, polycotton, nylon, viscose and blends. The wash cycle is gentler than cotton programmes so is suitable for more delicate items. Select a long pre-soak on this cycle so the cleaning can be achieved by means of the soaking process. The most common temperatures are 40°C (105°F) and 50°C (120°F).

Wool/Delicate Gentler still, this programme is usually pre-set at 40°C (105°F), but some machines now have a 30°C (85°F) cycle. Slow, short movement and spin on the delicate cycle protects your finest materials from friction and snags.

Other programmes and options include:

Anti-crease cycle The drum tumbles the load intermittently for up to 30 minutes after washing.

Drip dry/no spin Washes without spinning – useful for delicate items.

Economy options Reduces the wash temperature or length of the programme.

Extra rinse Good for people with sensitive skin as the extra water ensures all of the detergent is removed.

Freshen-up option This is a rinse with a fabric conditioner for delicate clothing.

Gentle/hand/silk washes Reduces the amount of agitation for delicate items.

Refresh programme Washes lightly soiled and delicate fabrics at 30°C (85°F).

Rinse hold/crease guard/delay spin The machine stops during the final rinse. Clothes are held in the water and the machine will not spin until it is reset. This reduces creasing.

Quick/rapid wash For lightly soiled loads.

Soak Clothes are soaked in water for up to two hours before washing.

Starch programme Allows you to add starch to soften and condition wet washing.

HAND-WASHING

The most delicate fabrics need to be washed by hand instead of in a washing machine. Always read the wash care label to check how an item should be washed. It is recommended to use a specialized detergent for hand-washing, which will be gentler on delicate fabrics than standard detergents. Such products are readily available from most supermarkets or online.

How to Wash by Hand

• Put some cool-to-tepid water in a sink or washing-up bowl and add some specialized hand-washing detergent (see the packaging for the recommended amount to use).

• Immerse the item to be washed in the water and leave to soak for several minutes.

• Do not squeeze or rub the item.

• Gently move the item back and forth through the water, then rinse thoroughly in cool, clear water.

• Do not wring. Instead, squeeze any excess water out gently by patting the item between two clean, colourfast towels.

• Dry the item flat or on a hanging rack. If hanging it on a rack with clips, make sure you don't clip the delicate parts of the item or you might stretch or damage it. Instead, loop the item around the clips.

NON-STANDARD WASHABLES

* Follow the care labels to determine whether you *wash by hand*, in a *machine* or *dry-clean*.

* Scrub *plastic shower curtains* with a sponge soaked in a solution made from detergent and hot water. To remove mildew, add a little bleach to the water or use an anti-mildew spray cleaner. Rinse thoroughly.

* Do not wash *suede* or lined *leather gloves*. Clean the outside with a soft, wet cloth, then clean with a proprietary leather and suede cleaner available from department stores or shoe retailers.

* *Wool gloves* can be machine washed on a wool cycle or hand-washed.

* To hand wash *lingerie* see page 25. To machine wash, put tights, stockings and other delicate items in a net lingerie bag. Fasten bras to prevent snagging (do not machine wash under-wired bras as the wire can damage the machine). Select the delicate/wool programme and use a non-biological detergent. Avoid chlorine bleach. Dry flat or on a hanging rack.

DETERGENTS, SOAPS AND WASHING AIDS

Buying a washing powder or detergent used to involve simply selecting a brand and size; now you have to choose between shelves of different products. Always read the instructions on the detergent and use as recommended, and test fabrics for colourfastness when using additives, see page 30.

Conventional powders These are for either machine or hand-washing (don't confuse the two: if hand-washing powder is used in a machine it will produce too much foam and harm the machine). The active ingredients include surfactants which attack dirt, builders that hold the dirt in the water, phosphates, bleaches and optical whiteners. There are two types of powder: biological and non-biological. Biological powders contain enzymes which help to break down stains at lower temperatures. Non-biological powders don't contain enzymes.

Mild/speciality detergents With a neutral or near-neutral pH, these work less well on stains than stronger detergents, but are best for use on delicate fabrics.

Pre-wash detergents These are great for removing heavy soiling either as a pre-soak before machine or hand-washing, or when used in a pre-wash programme.

Powders for coloureds These don't contain bleaches, so they won't fade or dull coloured fabrics. They can be biological or non-biological.

Tablets and pouches These reduce the risk of using too little or too much.

Liquid detergents When using in a machine, dispense these through the drawer or in a dosing ball. They tend to be gentler than powdered detergents.

Fabric softeners These will fluff up the material and reduce static cling and creasing to make ironing easier. Softeners can build up in the fibres and eventually become less effective. Avoid use in every wash. Don't use fabric softeners on flame-retardant garments, because they reduce the effectiveness of the special treatment.

Optical brighteners These are found in nearly all detergents and bleaches to make white or coloured material look crisper and brighter in daylight.

Whiteners/brighteners Continued washings can fade or alter the colour of clothes. Whiteners and brighteners will prevent fading, whiten whites and restore colour. They are available separately or as additives to laundry detergents.

Bleach Bleaching is a process by which dark or coloured pigments are made to dissolve in the wash. Chlorine bleaches whiten and disinfect material, but can strip fibres and discolour hues. They will damage silk, wool, leather, mohair, nylon, elastic, resin-treated and flame-retardant materials. Hydrogen peroxide, in diluted form, is an 'oxygen bleach', which is good for fine material, including washable white wool and silk. Oxygen bleach pre-treatment sticks are excellent and can be used on stains up to one week before the item is washed. Work the stick into the newly soiled area, then put the item in the basket/hamper until laundry day.

TESTING FOR COLOURFASTNESS

When you are washing a garment for the first time, especially a delicate item, always test for colourfastness before washing.

Whites

- Always wash whites separately from coloured items to avoid dye transfering onto the whites.
- Do not bleach delicate items which specifically state 'no bleach'.
- Chlorine bleach can bring out crisp whiteness and remove stubborn spots on white clothes.
- If your white clothes have a coloured trim, test the trim for colour change before using bleach (see opposite).

Colours

- Always separate dark colours from light ones before washing.
- Test for possible 'bleeding'. Materials to test are denim, tie-dyed clothes, hand-painted items and Indian gauzes.
- Fabrics that can continue to bleed are denim, and clothes coloured with madras and natural vegetable dyes.
- Always use a detergent recommended for coloured fabrics.

Detergent

To check whether a fabric is colourfast with your detergent, do the following test:

1. Add one teaspoon of detergent to 250 ml/1 cup of warm or hot water.

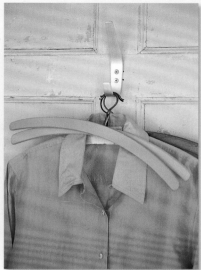

2. Immerse a corner of the garment in the solution.

3. Press onto a clean, white cloth, strong paper towels or tissues.

4. If nothing bleeds, then rinse, let dry and test again. If the fabric bleeds or the cloth is stained, dry-clean the garment.

Chlorine Bleach (Sodium Hypochlorite)

To test whether a garment is colourfast with chlorine bleach, carry out this test:

1. Add one tablespoon of bleach to 250 ml/1 cup of cool water and apply to a hidden underseam.

2. Wait at least one minute.

3. Dab with a clean, white cloth.

4. Check for yellowing.

5. After rinsing, dry, then check again.

Other Wash Additives

To test any other washing products, make a slightly stronger solution than normal by mixing it with just a small amount of water. Test as for detergent (see opposite).

STAIN REMOVAL

Stains are the bane of any laundry washer's life. They can ruin clothes and household linens, but a stain doesn't have to signal the end of a garment's life. There are hundreds of stain-removing products available, it's just a matter of finding the right one.

The Basics

• First check that the garment is neither hand-wash or dry-clean only.

• Read and follow pack instructions on all cleaning products.

• Treat stains as soon as possible as it is easier to remove new stains that haven't yet set into the fabric. If the item is dry-clean only, take it to be professionally dry-cleaned as soon as you can. Point out the stain to the dry-cleaner – mark it with a safety pin so you don't forget where it is.

• Test the stain remover on an unseen area of the item to check for colourfastness exactly as you would for a detergent (see page 30). Rinse.

• When using bleach, bleach the entire item to prevent uneven colour.

• Place the stained material face down on a clean cloth or absorbent paper towels when working to remove the stain.

• Put the stain remover on the reverse side of the stain.

• Dry-cleaning solvents should never go into your washing machine as they are flammable. Always rinse garments after applying such solvents and let them air dry before putting them in the washing machine.

• Use stain removers cautiously and separately.

• Always wash clothes after you have treated them with stain removers.

• If there is any bleach in the stain remover, be cautious and check the wash care label on the material you are treating to see if it is safe to use. If it isn't, try all-purpose or oxygen bleach instead.

COMMON STAINS

The 'oops' of eating, the stains from everyday use, the little accidents that happen when we work and play and the stains that result can ruin our clothes. However, the information below should give you a fighting chance. If the directions call for bleach, but your fabric is coloured, make sure you use a colour-safe bleach or a specific stain remover.

Cosmetics

Deodorants/antiperspirants Treat with a liquid detergent, then wash as normal. If more treatment is needed, use a pre-wash stain remover. Use a biological powder and in-wash stain remover.

Foundation Soak using a pre-wash detergent, then machine wash at as high a temperature as the fabric will allow. For stubborn marks, treat with a stain remover or liquid detergent: work into the dampened stain until the outline of the stain is gone, then rinse. If an oily spot persists, treat with a biological detergent. Rinse and wash as normal.

Lipstick Soak in a detergent solution, then dab with a proprietary stain remover. Sponge with a detergent solution, then wash as normal.

Nail polish This is very difficult to remove. However you can try nail polish remover (but never use it on synthetic fabrics). Place the stained garment, stain side down, on paper towels and soak with nail polish remover. Replace the paper towels frequently as the stain will run into it. Repeat until the stain is gone. Rinse, then wash as normal.

Environmental Stains

Grass First, treat with a proprietary grass stain remover. Then machine wash using a biological detergent.

Mud Let dry, then remove as much of the caked mud as possible. Wash at the hottest temperature allowed for the fabric using a biological powder and in-wash stain remover. Repeat the process if necessary.

Pollen To remove surface pollen, dab with adhesive tape or use a vacuum cleaner nozzle/tip on low suction. Treat with a proprietary grass stain remover, then wash as normal.

Everyday Stains

Collar and cuff soils Treat with a stain bar or specialist spray for collars and cuffs and let sit for 30 minutes, or longer, then wash as normal.

Dye run (white material that has picked up dye from another garment) Use a commercial colour run remover. Wash as normal. If the stain persists, soak the item in bleach and wash again. For coloured fabrics and delicate whites that cannot be bleached, soak in a biological detergent solution, then wash. To minimize dye transfers, remove items from the washing machine as soon as the programme is finished.

Mildew Treat old stains on white fabric with a bleach solution or a specialist stain remover for mould and mildew. If some soil persists, apply a hydrogen peroxide solution. Rinse and wash as normal. Let air dry in direct sunlight.

Perspiration Apply a proprietary stain remover. Wash in the hottest water allowed for the fabric in question. Pre-treat stubborn stains with a stain remover, then wash using a biological powder.

Yellowing of white cottons or linens Wash at as high a temperature as allowed for the fabric using a biological powder plus a proprietary whitening product (see pages 28–29).

Yellowing of white nylon Let the item sit overnight in a pre-wash product or 'oxygen bleach' (see page 29). Wash in hot water with a biological powder, checking the wash care symbol for the hottest water temperature recommended for the fabric you are treating.

Foods

Baby formula Soak the stain in a pre-wash detergent for a few hours. Run the item through the washing machine as normal.

Beverages (soft drinks, white wine, alcoholic drinks) Soak the stain in cool water. Rub stain remover or liquid laundry detergent into the spot, then wash with a biological powder.

Chocolate This should come out if you machine wash using a biological powder.

Coffee and tea (black or with sugar/sweetener) Run the stain under cool water immediately, if possible, then treat the stain with detergent and wash with a biological powder.

Coffee and tea (with milk only – no sugar) Sponge the stain with warm water. Apply liquid detergent, then wash in the hottest water allowed for the fabric, using a biological powder.

Dairy-based products Treat with a stain bar or soak in a pre-soak product for 30 minutes if the stain is fresh, or for several hours for older stains. After soaking, wash as normal.

Egg Make a solution from 150 g/¾ cup of biological powder per 4 litres/7 cups of cool water. Soak the stain in this solution for 30 minutes for a recent stain or for several hours for an older stain. Wash the garment as normal.

Fruit juices Soak the item in cool water and then treat with a proprietary fruit and wine stain remover. You might need to bleach white fabrics in order to get the best finish possible.

Tomato ketchup/sauce Rinse the item in cold water, then soak in a solution made from 150 g/¾ cup of detergent per 4 litres/7 cups of cool water for about 30 minutes. Wash as normal with a biological detergent.

Mustard First treat the spot with a pre-wash stain remover, then machine wash with a biological detergent.

Red wine Act immediately. Never cover the stain with salt as this will set the stain. A traditional solution is to pour on sparkling or soda water. Soak a clean, white cloth with water and douse the stain liberally with it. Then use a clean, dry cloth to blot dry. Treat dried stains with a stain remover or a solution of hydrogen peroxide.

Gum, Paints and Other Difficult Substances

Chewing gum or adhesive tape
Treat with ice to harden the matter for easy removal and rub off with the edge of a spatula. Saturate with stain remover. Rinse, then run through your washing machine as normal.

Grease (cooking oil and fats, motor oils) Light soil can be pre-treated with a spray stain remover, liquid washing detergent or a pre-wash product. Wash in the hottest water allowed for the material. Put ingrained spots face down on clean paper towels. Apply a proprietary stain remover to the back of the stain and change the paper towels regularly. Let air dry, then rinse. Wash the garment in the hottest water possible.

Paint A stain caused by water-based emulsion paint should be soaked in warm water before it sets, then wash as normal. This kind of stain most often cannot be treated when dry. For oil-based paints, including varnish, use the solvent listed on the label as thinner. If there is no label information, use turpentine. Rinse. Pre-treat with stain remover or detergent. Rinse and wash. This is very unlikely to be removed.

Rust Use a commercial rust and iron-mould remover. Treat straight away because it can spread to other garments.

Shoe polish To remove liquid shoe polish, apply a paste of powdered detergent and water, then wash. Use the edge of a spatula to remove any remaining shoe polish and paste from the material. Pre-treat with a stain remover, then rinse. Work in detergent to moisten the spot, then wash using a biological powder.

Tobacco Wet the spot and work in bar soap, then rinse. Use a stain bar or soak in a biological detergent solution. Wash as normal. If the spot persists, soak in a hydrogen peroxide solution and wash again.

Human Excretions

Blood Let a recently stained garment sit in cold water for one hour. Work liquid detergent into any remaining stain. Rinse, then wash. Treat a dried spot in a warm biological detergent solution, then wash as normal. If stain remains, wash again.

Urine, vomit, mucus or faeces Machine wash at as high a temperature as the fabric will allow using biological powder. If the odour persists after washing, use a fabric deodorizer.

Ink

Fountain pen ink Dab fresh stains with milk or hold them under cold running water until they have gone, then wash using a biological powder. Use bleach on older stains on white fabrics or a proprietary stain remover on coloured fabrics.

Ballpoint ink Put the spot face down on a white cloth to absorb most of the stain. Try holding the garment under cold running water until the pigments are gone. Rub liquid detergent into the stain, then rinse. Repeat if necessary. Soak in warm water and add 1–4 tablespoons of ammonia per 1 litre/1¾ cups of water. Rinse well. Wash at a high temperature and use bleach, if the fabric will allow it.

DRYING

Once you've washed your laundry, spin dry to remove as much water as possible. Line drying will give you the freshest smelling results, but a tumble dryer or drying rack is often most convenient, especially in wet weather.

TUMBLE DRYING

*Before you choose a tumble dryer, you need to consider where you will
put it. A condenser model can be sited anywhere as it doesn't have a hose.
A vented model has a hose that channels the steam outside via a hole in
a wall or through a window.*

The Basics

• It is best to underdry rather than overdry. More sophisticated sensor dryers
have moisture sensing strips or 'electronic drying' that automatically turn the
machine off when the required level of dryness is reached.

• Add enough items to provide proper tumbling, but never overfill the dryer.
You want proper ventilation to give even drying throughout, without wrinkling.
Full-sized dryers will dry a load of about 5 kg/11lbs.

• Clothes that require specific washing temperatures usually require similar drying
temperatures. Use the highest heat setting for cotton, denim and linens, a low or
delicate temperature setting for synthetics, fine knits and anything that will snag.

• Tumble dryers can wear off elastics and rubber on items such as fitted sheets.
You may want to line dry such items occasionally to prolong their life.

• It is important to check the lint filter and empty it after every load as too much
lint in your dryer can cause a fire. Empty the dryer hose once a year. To do this,
remove the hose from the machine and pass an old towel through it.

• If you have a condenser dryer empty the water container after each use.

• Remove items from the dryer as soon as the cycle has finished. The items should
still have a trace of dampness.

• Hang or fold items as soon as you take them out of the dryer to prevent wrinkles
forming. Have on hand a few plastic hangers on which to place or fold the clothes.

• To condition flat-dried clothes, 'air-fluff' them on a cool air setting. This will
prevent them from becoming stiff.

• If clean clothes are wrinkled, put them in the dryer with a moistened, lint-free
towel on a low temperature setting for 5–10 minutes.

DRYING FLAT

* Many knits and woollens have care labels indicating that the item needs to *'dry flat'.* If this is the case, make sure you do so otherwise you risk *stretching* or *mis-shaping* the fabric.

* Find a flat area *away from sunlight* and lay the item flat on a clean, well-pressed white sheet. Make sure the area is *well ventilated* and *away from pets* and *children*.

* Items dried flat often need to be *'air-dried' for 5 minutes* in the *tumble dryer* to prevent stiffness. Check the wash care symbol on the garment before putting it in the tumble dryer.

DRIP DRYING

* *Light cottons, polyesters, silk* and *items that do not stretch* can be hung to dry. Otherwise, dry flat.

* Hang *jackets, blouses, sweaters* and *dresses* (unless marked 'dry flat') on hangers that fit their shape and allow them to drape properly. Make sure the shoulders of the hangers are nicely rounded.

* Make sure you close *buttons* or *zips* correctly. Smooth *collars, seams, trim* and *pockets*.

* Use collapsible drying racks or a hanging rack for *lingerie, hosiery* and other items that do not need hangers.

LINE
DRYING

* Peg *bras* by the hooked end.

* Peg *dresses* by the shoulder.

* Peg *full skirts* by the hem.

* Peg *pillowcases* one side only, leaving the other side to hang open.

* Fold *sheets* hem to hem over the line and peg by the corners.

* Hang *shirts* by the tail and always unbuttoned

* Peg *socks* by the toe.

* Peg *straight skirts* and *trousers/pants* by the waistband.

* Peg *towels* at the corners after shaking.

* Peg *t-shirts* by the hem.

* Fold *underwear* over the line and peg.

IRONING & PRESSING

What more pleasing sight is there than a neatly folded pile of freshly-ironed laundry? With pristine clothes in your wardrobe/closet, clean sheets on the bed and fresh bathroom and dish towels on hand, you will feel revived and your home will look luxurious.

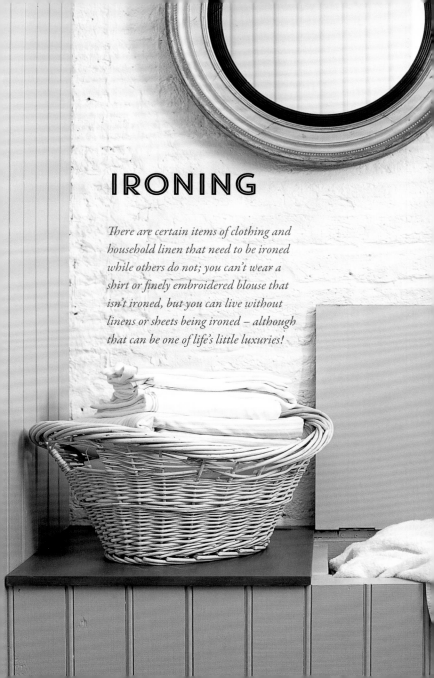

IRONING

There are certain items of clothing and household linen that need to be ironed while others do not; you can't wear a shirt or finely embroidered blouse that isn't ironed, but you can live without linens or sheets being ironed – although that can be one of life's little luxuries!

The Basics

- Make sure your ironing board is well padded and that the cover is clean.
- Your iron soleplate should be clean and residue/rust-free (see page 57).
- Wait until the iron is hot enough to steam the water before starting to iron.
- Check the wash care label and always use the correct temperature setting on the iron for the particular item.
- Test the heat on a hidden area of material first, such as the underside of a hem, to avoid scorching your garments.
- Put the item on the ironing board and flatten it out.
- Use one hand to keep the garment straight while the other hand moves the iron.
- Move the iron lightly but deliberately in a sliding motion over the fabric.
- Never leave the hot plate of the iron facing downwards. Always set the iron on its stand when you let it rest.
- Iron garments needing the lowest setting first and progress to those needing the highest. Use the one-dot setting for acrylic, silk, nylon polyamide, acetate and polyester; the two-dot setting for polyester blends and wool; and the three-dot setting for cotton, linen, viscose and denim.
- Iron thicker areas of the garment first in order to avoid creasing the thinner, more delicate parts as you continue to iron the rest of the garment.
- Have on hand a spray bottle or a sponge for sprinkling or dabbing water, and spraying starches.
- Cottons and linens should be sprinkled with water one hour before ironing. Iron while still damp, using a hot-steam iron setting. Flatwork should be sprinkled on one side only. Two-sided items, such as clothing and pillowcases, should be sprinkled on both sides.
- Press cotton and linen items while they are still slightly damp on a hot steam setting.
- Use a cool-steam iron setting on untreated cottons, viscose and silks.
- For minimum ironing, use perma-pressed clothes and blended fabrics. Remove from the dryer as soon as the programme has finished, fluff out and fold or hang the items neatly.
- Always hang or fold laundry as soon as it is dry to minimize the creases and therefore reduce your ironing load.

PRESSING

Delicate fabrics should be pressed rather than ironed to prevent them getting crushed, stretched, damaged or becoming shiny. Tailored suits as well as garments made from wool, silk, rayon, netting and pile fabrics should all be pressed rather than ironed.

The Basics

• Whereas ironing involves 'sliding' the iron across the fabric, pressing comprises of a press and lift technique. Press the iron onto the fabric, then lift it off quickly; avoid 'sliding' the iron as much as possible.

• A pressing cloth should be used to act as a heat buffer between the iron and the fabric. This can be made from unbleached muslin or cheesecloth or you can use a clean, white towel.

• When pressing delicate fabrics, put a heavy towel (without a nap) under the item. Press on the wrong side of the fabric, using a steam iron setting or a damp pressing cloth with your iron set at medium heat.

• Wrinkles should be steamed out.

IRONING TIPS

Here are some helpful hints to consider when ironing a variety of fabrics or garments with decorative features.

Creases Iron on the wrong side first, using small strokes on collars, hems and cuffs, while pressing out smoothly with the palm of your hand.

Damasks Iron both sides to produce a sheen on the top side.

Delicate fabrics To avoid creating a sheen on delicate fabrics, iron on the wrong side or use a clean dish towel as a pressing cloth. This applies to fabrics such as wool gabardine, polyester, linen and all silks.

Embroidered or sequined fabrics Lay the item face down on a dish towel, then iron on the wrong side with a pressing cloth over the top of the fabric to protect patterns and delicate areas.

Fringes Untangle while wet.

Gathers Iron from the outside into the gathers.

Lace and cutwork Use a pressing cloth or dish towel; don't put the iron directly on the lace.

Linen Sprinkle linen items with water, then stretch the damp linen into shape. Use a hot iron, but take care because linen can scorch quite easily. Iron on the wrong side to press the item into shape, but not to dry it. Stop ironing while there is still a suggestion of dampness in the fabric. Over-drying will increase the chance of scorching. Never iron on the right side. Hang immediately to finish drying naturally.

Napkins Iron flat. Do not iron creases, these should be pressed instead.

Pile fabrics These fabrics should not be ironed.

Plackets Close zips, poppers and hooks, but not buttons, before ironing plackets. Work the iron carefully around any buttons, hooks, poppers or zips.

Pleats Lay or pin the pleats in place before ironing. Hold the material taut against the pressure of the iron. Iron in long strokes starting at the waist and working down to the hem.

Puffed sleeves Stuff puffed sleeves or pockets with tissue paper or a small towel before ironing.

Sheets Fold flat sheets in half, iron, then fold completely. There is no need to iron fitted sheets because they are pulled tightly over the corners of the mattress and any creases will disappear.

Stretchy fabrics Put a pressing cloth on top of the fabric and iron in the direction of the weave.

Tablecloths Round ones should be ironed in a circular motion, turning the fabric around as you iron. Fold square or rectangular tablecloths in half, wrong side facing out. Sprinkle with water, then iron until half dry; refold with right side facing out and iron until nearly dry. Press out any creases when both sides are finished.

IRON CARE

* Let your iron *air dry to cool*. Give it plenty of time and don't be impatient.

* If starch sticks to the soleplate, wait for the iron to cool completely, then apply a mixture of *one part bicarbonate of/baking soda* to *one part water*. Leave for 15 minutes, then work off with a moist cloth. Alternatively use a proprietary soleplate cleaner.

* Mineral deposits develop with time inside the iron's water tank. To remove them, pour some *white vinegar* inside and *allow the iron to steam* for *five minutes,* but check the manufacturer's instructions first. Iron a clean cloth to bring out any residues. Let the iron cool, then rinse the tank with cold water.

* Always empty out the water after each use.

* Most manufacturers claim you can use *tap water* in your iron but it will speed up the build up of limescale. Prevent this by using filtered/distilled water.

* Clean any *anti-scale* devices as recommended by the manufacturer.

FOLDING

A little time taken to care for clothes and linens is time well spent. Once they have been washed and ironed, it's worth folding them correctly so they fit in your drawers, dressers and cupboards easily, without getting crumpled.

CLOTHING

If you fold your clothes carefully you will set the folds in the right places and prevent them getting creased in your drawers or on your shelves. Follow the simple instructions below to achieve the best results for your clothes.

Dresses It is advisable to hang dresses in a wardrobe/closet. But if you can't, fold them at the waist, then tuck the sleeves in like a shirt (see below). Bring the edges of the skirt together carefully. If the skirt is long, fold it up, but not in the middle.

Handkerchiefs Fold handkerchiefs in a square after pressing.

Lingerie Divide into three separate drawers – or into three compartments within a large drawer – one for knickers/pants, one for bras and one for hosiery. Each should be separated by colour with knickers/pants folded like underpants (see opposite) and bras cup-side up. Previously worn tights and stockings should be stored according to colour and thickness and folded into fourths. Put scented sachets with these to keep them sweet-smelling.

Shirts Button the first, middle and last buttons or poppers and set the shirt face down. Bring one sleeve across the back of the shirt horizontally, folding the shoulder over, too. Fold the sleeve down vertically at the shoulder area. Repeat

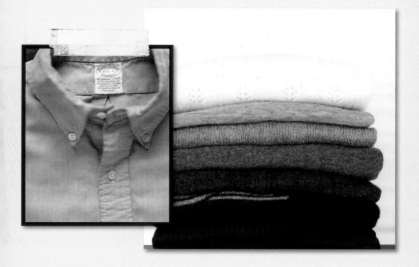

with the other sleeve. Fold the lower third up, then fold the next third up. Turn the shirt face upwards. Put away carefully in a drawer or on a shelf.

Shorts First, make sure any pockets have been carefully flattened. Align the inseams and try to lay the shorts out evenly in a drawer. If you must fold them, do so carefully in half.

Skirts It is always better to hang up a skirt, either on a clip hanger or by its own loops. If you aren't able to do so, bring the edges of the skirt together. If the skirt is long, fold it up, but avoid folding it in the middle.

Socks Never roll socks up into a ball as this stretches one sock, ruining its elastic and takes up too much room in the drawer. Instead, put one sock on top of the other and fold them neatly together in half.

Trousers and jeans Use trouser hangers, if you can. Hang the trousers carefully by the bottom hems, making sure you align the inseams. If you don't have trouser hangers, use thick, wooden hangers and fold them over the hanger, again making sure to align the inseams.

Underpants Lay them out flat. Fold each side towards the middle, then fold them up in half.

HOUSEHOLD LINEN

When folding more sizeable items, such as sheets, duvet covers and large tablecloths, the task is made much easier and the result is much neater if accomplished by two people. If you do have to do it on your own, lay the items on the bed and fold them there.

Blankets Fold in half from bottom to top, then in half again from left to right. Flip the blanket over and fold again.

Duvets/Comforters To store, put the duvet in washed, unbleached muslin or cotton. Use tissue paper between the folds and store in an acid-free box or on a shelf lined with cotton sheeting. You can buy storage bags for duvets/comforters and blankets. Never use plastic bags because they lock in moisture. To prevent mould and mildew, duvets/comforters must not be stored in a humid room, such as the bathroom. Heating units and direct sunlight can ruin your duvet/comforter.

Fitted sheets Make sure both top corners of the sheet are puffed out. Fold the sheet in half from bottom to top. Fit the bottom two corners into the top two corners. Make the sides of the sheet perfectly even by laying it flat on the bed and smoothing down. Fold in half again from bottom to top, then fold from left to right. Lay the sheet neatly on a shelf, tamping down in order to prevent creases.

Flat sheets Match the bottom edges to the top edges and fold in half, with the top side of the sheet facing out. Fold in half from bottom to top again, then fold in half from left to right. Larger sheets may need to be folded one more time so that they fit on the shelf. Lay your fitted sheets on top of your flat sheets.

Napkins Store these in an acid-free container or on shelves covered with cotton sheeting. Never iron in creases, or mould may develop. Fold loosely into a square or rectangle, with the monogram (if applicable) on the lower left-hand corner.

Pillowcases Fold in half lengthways, then in half widthways.

Tablecloths Store linen tablecloths wrapped in acid-free paper. Like napkins, keep them either in an acid-free container or on shelves covered with cotton sheeting. Be sure to refold them frequently to prevent mould and creasing.

Towels Fold in thirds lengthways, then in half or thirds widthways.

INDEX

PICTURE CREDITS

ph = photographer

endpapers ph Lucinda Symons; **1** Signe Bindslev Henriksen of Space Architecture and Design. ph Winfried Heinze; **2** Available for location hire at *shootspaces.com*. ph Debi Treloar; **3** ph Sandra Lane; **4** ph Polly Wreford; **5 left** The home of Patty Collister in London, owner of An Angel At My Table. ph Debi Treloar; **5 right** ph Polly Wreford; **6** The home of Ilaria of IDA Interior Lifestyle in Eindhoven. ph Rachel Whiting; **8–9** ph Henry Bourne; **11** ph Polly Wreford; **12 above left** ph Polly Wreford; **12 above right** ph Claire Richardson; **12 below** Jane Moran's cottage in Sussex. ph Jan Baldwin; **13** Kate Forman's home. ph Lisa Cohen; **14** ph Andrew Wood; **16–17** stylist Rose Hammick and architect Andrew Treverton's home in London. ph Dan Duchars; **18** Anna Mcdougall's London Home. ph Lisa Cohen; **19** ph Andrew Wood; **20** ph Kristin Perers; **23** ph Dan Duchars; **24 background** The family home of designers Ulla Koskinen & Sameli Rantanen in Finland. ph Debi Treloar; **24 insert** ph Lucinda Symons; **25** The family home of Nicky Sanderson, the co-owner of Lavender Room in Brighton, East Sussex. ph Debi Treloar; **26** ph Sandra Lane; **27** Josephine Ryan's house in London. ph Claire Richardson; **29** ph Claire Richardson; **31 left** ph Holly Jolliffe; **31 right** ph Debi Treloar; **32** The London home of

designer Kathy Dalwood *kathydalwood.com* and artist Justin Mortimer *justinmortimer.co.uk*. ph Debi Treloar; **34** ph Polly Wreford; **35** ph Claire Richardson; **36** ph Kate Whitaker; **37** ph Alan Williams; **39 above left** ph Winfried Heinze; **39 above right** ph Kristin Perers; **39 below** left ph Polly Wreford; **39 below right** The designer Clare Teed's home in Hampton, *sashawaddell.com*. ph Lisa Cohen; **40–41** ph Chris Tubbs; **43 above left** ph James Merrell; **43 above right** ph Chris Tubbs; **43 below left** ph Chris Tubbs; **43 below right** ph Holly Jolliffe; **44** ph Polly Wreford; **46 left** ph Claire Richardson; **46 right** ph Mark Lohman; **47** ph Mark Lohman; **48–49** the home of Ilaria of IDA Interior Lifestyle in Eindhoven. ph Rachel Whiting; **50** stylist Rose Hammick and architect Andrew Treverton's home in London. ph Dan Duchars; **52** ph Claire Richardson; **53** ph Andrew Wood; **55** ph Kristin Perers; **56** Mark & Sally Bailey's home in Herefordshire. ph Debi Treloar; **57** The home of the designer Edith Mezard in Lumieres. ph Debi Treloar; **58–60** ph Polly Wreford; **61 left** ph Kristin Perers; **61 right** ph Polly Wreford; **62** ph Mark Scott; **63** ph Polly Wreford; **64** ph Debi Treloar.